T0131571

"For Such a Time as This"

-ESTHER 4:14

A Caregiver's Encouragement

CAROLYN HARRISON

WESTBOW
PRESS®
A DIVISION OF THOMAS NELSON
& ZONDERVAN

WestBow Press books may be ordered through booksellers or by contacting:

WestBow Press
A Division of Thomas Nelson & Zondervan
1663 Liberty Drive
Bloomington, IN 47403
www.westbowpress.com
844-714-3454

Interior Image Credit: Russell Robards

ISBN: 978-1-6642-8961-1 (sc)
ISBN: 978-1-6642-8962-8 (hc)
ISBN: 978-1-6642-8960-4 (e)

Library of Congress Control Number: 2023900970

Print information available on the last page.

WestBow Press rev. date: 10/20/2023

In Loving Memory

This is an aged, black-and-white photograph of my beloved mother, Olga Hill, in LaGrange, Georgia, in her late twenties.

If I could touch you, my beloved mother,
If I could hear your voice calling my name,
If I could gaze upon your beautiful face,

Everything about you, my beloved mother,
Is a blessing and a pleasure.

May your enduring, heartfelt memories be
eternally cherished in the pages of this book.

To my husband, Charlie Harrison
For your sincere and constant love for my beloved mother

Let's not merely say that we love each other;
let us show the truth by our actions.
—1 John 3:18 (NLT)

Contents

Preface

Those who know your name trust in you, for you,
LORD, have never forsaken those who seek you.
—Psalm 9:10 (NIV)

The Holy Spirit guided me to study a few biblical examples in the Bible where God called and used individuals to execute His plan. Some of them were just like me—fearful, faithless, imperfect, inexperienced, and inadequate. He used me in an area that was unfamiliar to me. I peered at my deficiencies and limitations. Do you know how I felt? I was petrified. I contemplated on some of the "un-" words—unqualified, unschooled, unskilled, and untrained. Does God think like me? No. He was not interested in my credentials, expertise, training, or knowledge. He had a plan. He called me to be a caregiver. *I am going to be an amateur caregiver*, I thought.

> For my thoughts are not your thoughts, neither
> are your ways my ways, saith the LORD. (Isaiah
> 55:8 KJV)
>
> For as the heavens are higher than the earth,
> so are my ways higher than your ways, and my
> thoughts than your thoughts. (Isaiah 55:9 KJV)

In my finite mind, I could not comprehend what God was about to do in my life. He had a plan and a purpose.

> And we know that all things work together for
> good to them that love God, to them who are
> the called according to his purpose. (Romans
> 8:28 KJV)

God took me on an incredible journey with Him. There were no detours, no exits, and no turning back, but there was proceeding forward with my eyes fixed in a steady and focused manner on Him. My path was tedious and complicated at times. During those periods, the Holy Spirit guided me to the Bible.

> Wait on the LORD: be of good courage, and he shall strengthen thine heart: wait, I say, on the LORD. (Psalm 27:14 KJV)

> My grace is all you need. My power works best in weakness. (2 Corinthians 12:9 NLT)

> Trust in the LORD with all your heart and lean not on your own understanding. (Proverbs 3:5 NIV)

> In all thy ways acknowledge him, and he shall direct thy paths. (Proverbs 3:6 KJV)

> I will never leave you. (Hebrews 13:5 CSB)

While meditating on God's Word, I stated with confidence I could do all things through Christ who gives me strength (Philippians 4:13). Only He could give me what I needed to sustain my circumstances. What was more, I had the indwelling Holy Spirit to assist me and empower me to do what He had called me to do.

When God called Moses to be the deliverer of Israel from Egypt, Moses raised several objections, but God ejected them. I read one of the objections: Moses asked the question, "Who am I to go to the king and lead your people out of Egypt?" (Exodus 3:11 CEV). God did not answer the question Moses asked. Instead, He replied, "I will be with you" (Exodus 3:12 CEV). Then I meditated on what God told Joshua: "I will be with you; I will never leave you nor forsake you" (Joshua 1:5 NIV). I relied on the Holy Spirit to help me overcome my fears, and I trusted God's promises. I began my calling trusting in the Lord, trusting in His sovereignty and resting in His faithfulness. I did not know what lay ahead, but He knew. He is omniscient and knows everything. He promised He would never leave me or forsake me (Hebrews 13:5). He promised to be with me always (Matthew 28:20).

Never alone;
God walks with me.

Never alone;
His Spirit dwells in me.

Not forsaken;
He is there.

He is close,
He lives within.
I never walk alone.

Acknowledgments

I give thanks to you, O Lord my God,
with my whole heart, and I will
glorify your name forever.
—Psalm 86:12 (ESV)

Writing a book for the first time is challenging, but the experience is more rewarding than I could ever envision. The Holy Spirit was my greatest guide. He gave me wisdom and knowledge.

I am filled with gratitude that WestBow Press chose to invest in this book, select it for publication, and market it to readers all over the world. Thank you, Brian Fox, for your consultation and professionalism. I acknowledge you, Juvy Luzon, Andre Trent, Lucas Biery, and Joe Anderson, for your forbearance and knowledge.

Thank you, Bob DeGroff, for your expertise, integrity, and assistance.

Thanks so much, Charlie Harrison, for being there for the joyful times and for the complex ones. Your selflessness will always be remembered and cherished.

I thank God for you, Lonnie Jr., Wilhelminia, and Margaret, for your prayers, uplifting words, support, and confidence in me to take care of our beloved mother, Olga. Our dad, Lonnie Sr., would have been pleased.

I wish to thank you, Frank Brown and Ruth Williams, for your loyalty. You are greatly appreciated.

Special thanks to you, Russell Robards, for your powerful prayers, dependability, expertise, reading numerous drafts, inspiration, design, layout, editing, mesmerizing cover, and masterful photography. You went above and beyond. Therefore, I am touched and filled with gratitude. Your light is shining (Matthew 5:16).

I am so grateful to you, Sarah T. Perry, for your outstanding editing skills and valuable time. I treasure your friendship, zeal for the Word of God, and love for Jesus Christ. Your support means much to me.

God provided exemplary healthcare professionals to assist me during my incredible, caregiving journey. The professionals spent quality time teaching and training me with love and care—thanks. With all sincerity, I applaud you.

How would I have made it through my incredible, caregiving journey without You, Lord? You gave me the best. I continue to thank You for being with me then and always. I love You so much!

Thank you, the reader, for taking the time to read my story. I pray you were encouraged and empowered, and you found peace in Jesus Christ.

God favored me to fulfill His purpose by penning this book. He is my greatest endorser.

Introduction

Do not fear, for I am with you; do not be afraid; for I
am your God. I will strengthen you; I will help you; I
will hold on to you with my righteous right hand.
—Isaiah 41:10 (CSB)

On the morning of February 18, 2003, I awoke with immense
fear and doubt. My heart was filled with great apprehension.
Suddenly, I experienced a moment of realization: *I am a caregiver.*

Life is filled with many unknowns. The magnitude of those
unknowns increases when they impact those we love. A myriad
of questions flooded my mind, which caused me to begin to
doubt my suitability for this journey. To whom could I turn to
sustain me as I began this journey with my precious loved one?

When life is calm, espousing religious rhetoric is easy. However,
it is amid trials and adversity we are compelled to employ
the principles of God's Word to lead us along this journey.
These principles empowered me with the strength I needed to
victoriously overcome my doubts and uncertainty.

As I daily observed the shining example who gave me life swiftly
fading, I began to realize it was God's will for the two of us to
suffer the pangs of love together. I knew her departure from this
earth would not be an expeditious transition, so I desired to do
everything I possibly could for my precious loved one. On numerous
occasions, I felt gravely inadequate for the task. But God!

It was during these times I humbled myself and offered the
best sacrifice I had to the only One who could help me. When
I surrendered all my inadequacies and lack of wisdom to Him,
He reassured me we were not alone as we walked this journey
together. Because of His mercy and grace, I performed many

acts of love for my precious loved one with tear-filled eyes, aching muscles, and a heavy heart.

Throughout my incredible journey as a caregiver, I discovered God was greater than all my doubts and fears. I gained a greater understanding of God's grace and a broader understanding of who He truly is.

As you read the pages of this book, I hope you are encouraged and empowered. Let Almighty God captivate you with powerful Bible verses, original poems, and specific guidance addressed to you. Relax by reading the Bible verses silently and audibly. Then, study and mediate on them. I invite you to use your Bible and take notes.

I often used three forceful words: pray, thank, and trust. These powerful words were essential to my caregiving journey. They intensified and strengthened my relationship with God and drew me closer to Him. His Word exhorted me to pray without ceasing (1 Thessalonians 5:17). His Word encouraged me to give thanks in all circumstances (1 Thessalonians 5:18). His Word commanded me to trust in Him (Proverbs 3:5).

I am captivated and grateful that you are going to take this incredible journey with me. As God—through the Holy Spirit—leads the way, let Him open your heart and mind with encouragement from the Word; grant you rest from worrying; mature your faith; enhance your trust in Him; provide you strength in weakness; teach you to pray; help you to be thankful; fill you with love, joy, and peace; draw you closer to Him; and give you hope through Jesus Christ.

Although this book is penned for caregivers, I pray that it not be shunned by others. It is a must read for all readers. Our life circumstances, challenges, and callings may be dissimilar, but we share the same Creator—Elohim (God).

May God empower you to accomplish His will through you and grant you peace "which transcends all understanding" (Philippians 4:7 NIV).

Part One

MY STORY

Commit everything you do to the LORD.
Trust him, and he will help you.
—Psalm 37:5 (NLT)

1

Commencing Years

2003–2008

After the demise of my loving dad, Lonnie Hill Sr., my beloved mother, Olga Hill, came to reside with me in 2003. She adjusted well to the changes; however, she missed her companion immensely. She was a sweet, considerate, and godly mother. She loved and feared the Lord. It was apparent in her life and conversation. I recall how she memorized Bible verses and recited them in joyous and intricate times. She practiced prayer and the Word of God in her life from day to day.

I adopted Mother's dogs, Precious and Reggie. She adored her energetic, handsome dogs. How could I say no to her? Each morning, she peered out of the bedroom window and engaged in a conversation with them. They stared at her in amazement and listened to what she was saying. When they barked, I assumed they concurred with what she was saying. She treasured those precious moments.

After communicating with Precious and Reggie, Mother prayed and read her Bible. Then she waited—each morning—with enthusiasm for a telephone call from my siblings, Lonnie Jr., Wilhelminia, and Margaret. Following that, she proceeded to the bathroom to get ready for that day. She dressed herself as if she were going to work. Lipstick was of the utmost importance. Although Mother was beautiful externally, her inner beauty, her character, is what made her a gorgeous woman. She always acknowledged the Lord in everything she did. Her mantra was, "If the Lord wills."

Before relaxing, Mother continued to the kitchen, where she cooked and ate breakfast. She spent a substantial amount of time there reflecting, remembering, and creating. Of course, this was her favorite room in the house. Her brand-new creations came alive in the kitchen—meats, vegetables, casseroles, breads, and desserts. She did not write her recipes on paper, but she shared them with my husband, Charlie, not me; she knew I was not fond of preparing meals. I would hear them in the kitchen laughing and exchanging information. My heart overflowed with joy. I remember those golden-brown miniature biscuits Mother prepared. She knew I savored hot buttered biscuits with syrup. Can you imagine eating fried chicken, fried pork chops, fried steaks, rice, gravy, and biscuits for breakfast? She took great pleasure in frying, baking, and roasting. She was a superb culinarian.

In the late afternoon, Mother hung out in the yard. She possessed a passion for gardening, particularly planting and pruning the flowers and shrubs. She had the time of her life working—with her lipstick on—and socializing with Precious and Reggie. Charlie knew she enjoyed being outside in the yard. He decided to plant a small vegetable garden for her pleasure. The garden reminded her of Dad and of her home in LaGrange, Georgia.

At the conclusion of the day, Mother and I spent special and cherished moments together praying, holding hands, expressing our affection, laughing, watching television, and conversing about Dad. We both loved and missed his presence. Those pleasant, sweet times satisfied us. I knew I could not fill the void in her life, but I attempted to make my home her home. She loved me, and I adored and respected her with all my heart. She was my mother. Her light shined as my example, my role model, my rock. I hold her teachings close. The days, weeks, months, and years spent chatting, holding hands, laughing, traveling, dining out, shopping, praying together, and discussing God's Word are priceless memories.

When Mother first came to live with me, I was still employed and knew we had to converse about procedures to follow in case of emergencies. She posted telephone numbers near the phone in her bedroom. She called me during the day, and I called her. Mother had cared for and nurtured me; now the roles were reversed. I thought, *Lord, help me to mimic her.*

I enjoy reminiscing on my early childhood years in LaGrange, Georgia. I recall how Mother taught my siblings and me to pray. One night a week, we all had to pray together as a family on our knees. Mother initiated the prayers, and then we had to pray. She did not tell us what to pray. We listened faithfully to her prayers. She was a powerful example. Dad worked at night, but we did see him on his knees praying. In our house, we knew God was first and Dad was next. Mother never diminished Dad's role.

Family meals together were revered. I respected them a lot. Dad was seated at the head of the table. After he blessed the food, we had to recite a Bible verse. Mother said it was okay for us to repeat the same verse over and over again. After a while, I grew weary of repeating "Jesus wept" (John 11:35 KJV), "Thou shalt not steal" (Exodus 20:15 KJV), and "Thou shalt not kill" (Exodus 20:13 KJV), so I memorized other Bible verses. Her teachings taught me the importance of praying and hiding God's Word in my heart. How clever she was!

My siblings and I were given a nickel and sometimes a dime for Sunday school and church. As adolescents, we received fifty cents. Finally, we reached one whole dollar. We had arrived. Dad and Mother taught us about loving, giving, and thanksgiving. We observed them. My parents had encumbrances, but they knew the Lord.

As I reflect with nostalgia on my childhood, adulthood, and now my senior years, the memories are countless and unforgettable. I cherish them with my heart and soul.

Cherishing your memories, my beloved.
They are all I have left of you.

Days and nights
Reminiscing,
Indulging in enjoyable moments of you.

The joyful times,
Your enduring love,
Your strong faith,
The wisdom you so often shared.

I still hear your singing in church,
Out of tune but praising the Lord.

Those gorgeous eyes,
Charming smile,
Not forgotten.

Deeply missed,
Forever loved,
My beloved.

One day, as Mother and I sat in her room at my home in Chattanooga, she read Dad's obituary. She said, "I miss Lonnie."

Then I made a surprising statement. "We are going to LaGrange in the spring." Her face lit up. She was ecstatic!

During late spring in 2003, Charlie, Mother, and I traveled to LaGrange, Georgia, to her home. She was elated and beaming. Charlie parked the car near the front porch. Mother's eyes were fixed on her house, flowers, and yard. She was exhilarated and thanked the Lord again and again. She did not wait for Charlie to open the door—she leaped out of the car and strolled to her flowers, pruning and talking to them. After she entered her house, she moved from room to room, making comments and expressing gratitude to the Lord.

The next day, Margaret drove to LaGrange to be with us. We had a marvelous retreat in the country. We planned our agenda for each day and waited until the late afternoon to give Mother a chance to complete her chores and care for her flowers. Thereafter, she would be ready to dine out at her favorite restaurant. Her visits to her home were filled with joy and serenity.

My siblings and I tried to do all we could to keep Mother actively involved with her church family and friends. She and I traveled to LaGrange on special holidays. From time to time, we would spend a week in LaGrange during spring break. She loved this time of the year because of her flowers. The beauty of each flower mesmerized her.

On certain occasions, Margaret vacationed in Chattanooga. We arranged a relaxing haven for Mother, lodged in a grand hotel, and pampered her. She did not adjust well to the hotel setting and preferred being at home. Margaret and I decided all her time should be spent at home, where she found joy and peace.

Now and then, Wilhelminia and her spouse, Frank, traveled to Chattanooga to accompany Mother to LaGrange for church revival. She appreciated the vigorous sermons and warm fellowship with her church family and friends. Lonnie Jr. made periodic visits to Chattanooga on weekends to escort Mother to church in LaGrange, along with Margaret. We enjoyed spoiling her. She was our mother—a godly mother.

Sincere
Loving
Compassionate
Prayerful
Devoted
Patient
Trustworthy
Diligent
Provider
Generous
Strong
Wisdom
God fearing
Bible believing

Her children rise up and call her blessed. (Proverbs 31:28 NKJV)

As time progressed, Mother lost interest in managing her personal business. Lonnie Jr. obtained an attorney and conveyed to her the importance of having a power of attorney. She agreed. *What is she thinking?* I wondered. She signed the legal documents with faith. Within her heart, she knew God was going to take care of her. I made a concerted effort to know where her business documents were located—insurance, deed, property taxes, and will. I shared the location of her business papers with my spouse and my siblings. God gave me wisdom to make wise decisions about her care and finances.

> If any of you lack wisdom, let him ask of God ... But let him ask in faith, nothing wavering. (James 1:5–6 KJV)

Caregivers, you need to know where your loved one's essential documents are located. Keep them in a safe location. A safe deposit box is one example. When Mother named me to be her power attorney, she had no doubts. She knew God was in control. I strove to be an excellent steward over her finances and care. Be prudent. Ask God to help you. In my own strength, I was powerless. I yielded to Him.

I look to You, Lord,
For my help comes from You.

I face nothing alone;
You are always with me.

I trust and acknowledge You,
For my strength comes from You.

I come to You and rest,
For my help comes from You.

Early in 2008, Mother's health began to decline. Leaving her at home unsupervised was no longer an option. I wanted to retire and care for her, but I felt financially insecure and fearful. I asked the Holy Spirit for guidance, and I prayed and meditated on God's Word. The following Bible verses resonated in my mind without ceasing.

> I am the LORD your God. I am holding your hand, so don't be afraid. I am here to help you. (Isaiah 41:13 CEV)

> When I am afraid, I will trust in you. (Psalm 56:3 CSB)

> For God hath not given us the spirit of fear; but of power, and of love, and of a sound mind. (2 Timothy 1:7 KJV)

> And my God will supply all your needs according to His riches in glory in Christ Jesus. (Philippians 4:19 NASB)

> Trust in Him at all times. (Psalm 62:8 NKJV)

God protected and kept Mother healthy until I could retire joyfully and thankfully in 2008 to care for her at age 55. I am beholden to God for His faithfulness and am blissful I trusted Him.

Trusting You, Lord,
To be with me.

Trusting You
To provide for me.

Trusting You
To take care of me.

You promised;
I believe.

God's way is perfect. All the LORD's promises prove true. (Psalm 18:30 NLT)

Rejoice always, pray continually, give thanks in all circumstances; for this is God's will for you in Christ Jesus.
—1 Thessalonians 5:16–18 NIV

2

Progressive Years

2009–2012

As she advanced in years, Mother's communication skills diminished. It pained me when she made an effort to share information with me. When she spoke, she gazed at me. Instead of speaking to her, I held her hand, massaging it over and over again.

One morning, during Mother's walk in the house, she fell. The falling incident frightened me. I called 911, and she was transported to the emergency room. Upon arrival, she was taken to a room where several tests were done. After the tests were completed, the physician stated she was fine, and I should follow up with her primary care doctor. *Thank you, Lord, for protecting Mother*, I prayed.

The falling incident made me conscious of Mother's unsteadiness. She continued to walk for exercise, but I assisted her. I noticed her knees and legs were becoming weaker. When she sat down, she had a difficult time getting out of the chair. Charlie did his best to teach me how to lift and support her, so we practiced these skills day and night. I made mistakes, but I kept my eyes focused on the Lord.

Lord, help me this day.
Guide me this day.
Show me this day.
Trusting You this day,
One day at a time.

Yesterday's past
Never to return.
Tomorrow is unrevealed.
Trusting You, Lord,
One day at a time.

Caregivers, taking one day at a time will help relieve some stress. Try not to concentrate on yesterday's errors, and don't worry about tomorrow's cares. Ask God to help you live one day at a time—leaning, depending, and trusting in Him.

Planning for tomorrow is time well spent; worrying about tomorrow is time wasted. (Matthew 6:34 NASB note)

Soon, the wedding celebration of Mother's grandson was approaching in Garner, North Carolina. Lonnie Jr. drove to Chattanooga to accommodate Mother and me. On an early summer morning, my brother, my beloved mother, and I traveled to the wedding. My brother did all the driving, and Mother and I relaxed by enjoying the spectacular mountain views.

The festivity was filled with so much love, cheerfulness, laughter, and fun. Mother kept late hours and enjoyed the social gathering. However, one person was missing: Dad. Tears flowed from my eyes without interruption. Oh, how I missed him. He was the head of the family—strong, provider, smart, God-fearing, generous, and humorous. My cherished memories of him will never cease. His memories will always live with me in my heart.

One month later, Margaret and I planned a weekend getaway to LaGrange, Georgia. We knew Mother would be elated, but she was withdrawn and disengaged. She showed no interest in her flowers, yard, or house. We felt melancholy and knew the traveling would come to an end.

Lonnie Jr., Wilhelminia, and Margaret continued to visit Mother in Chattanooga. When she heard their voices, it was heartfelt. Her eyes were fixed on them. She recognized them but could not call their names. They embraced her and expressed their love over and over—*I love you! I love you! I love you!* They had various times to assist and support me. Wilhelminia and her spouse, Frank, visited Mother during the Christmas holidays. They decorated and prepared meals. On Christmas morning, we showered Mother with gifts and affection. She was always the center of attention. Margaret made certain that I had a vacation or a weekend escape. She relieved me and cared for Mother. Whenever my sisters and I vacationed together, Mother resided with Lonnie Jr. in Southfield, Michigan.

Caregivers, it is necessary to have and use a support system. Do not isolate yourself. Use the resources provided by AARP in this book. There are numerous organizations and agencies listed to give assistance to you. Consult God for directions. Ask Him for whatever you need (Matthew 7:7) and believe (Mark 11:23; James 1:6). There is nothing God cannot achieve, execute, and conclude triumphantly. He is God.

No circumstance,
No problem,
No trial,
No situation

Too complicated
For God.

Ask,
Believe,
And receive.

In 2010, Lonnie Jr., Wilhelminia, Margaret, and I made a decision to honor Mother with a weekend of celebration commemorating her life. We lodged in an upscale hotel downtown Chattanooga. We seized all the splendor and artistry of the city.

Mother's banquet happened in a nineteenth-century Victorian home lavished with exquisite, impressive antiques. We experienced the historical elegance of the home. Guests and family members waited for Mother's appearance. Upon her arrival, all eyes were fixated on her. The room was filled with excitement and laughter. As always, she was the center of attention. The appetizing aroma of the food stimulated our appetites. We were ready for the blessing of the food so we could savor the main course meal and the mouthwatering desserts. After dinner, my siblings and I gave praise and thanks to God for His faithfulness and resources to honor our Mother. Then we paid tribute to our beloved mother, a godly woman. Naturally, our deceased dad's name was brought up throughout the banquet; it was impossible to honor her without him. We gave Mother kisses, hugs, cards, roses, and much love. To conclude the evening, a renowned singer serenaded Mother and us with music and songs. He made powerful statements about a godly mother and closed in prayer. What an awesome evening of celebration, joy, warmth, love, and commendation! The evening celebration was astounding. *Thank You, Father,* I proclaimed.

On a Saturday morning, the celebration continued for the family. Breakfast was served in one of the dining rooms in the hotel. We proudly wore our T-shirts to breakfast; Mother's name and year of birth were written on them. When she entered the room, the reception was passionate and deeply felt. She was greeted with respect and love. After Lonnie Jr. blessed the food, we ate and conversed with each other. My siblings and some of the grandchildren spoke at the breakfast. They shared powerful expressions about Dad and Mother's faith, love for God, and love for family. Each one of them expressed the impact Dad and Mother had made in their lives. The grandchildren remembered Mother's mantra, "If the Lord wills." Her mantra has been passed on to her children and grandchildren. Today,

I use it in my life faithfully. As anticipated, my siblings shared with the grandchildren how we were raised. Lonnie Jr. closed the breakfast with an emotional message to the grandchildren.

On Saturday evening, the family and relatives cruised down the Tennessee River on the renowned *Southern Belle* riverboat. The food was delicious, and the entertainment was superb. We captured striking sceneries of Chattanooga aboard the *Southern Belle*. Everyone had a fabulous time. Mother did not attend this event; Charlie cared for her at the hotel.

Family and relatives shared a wonderful time at Mother's celebration. It all climaxed on an early Sunday morning. Before departing the hotel, my siblings and their children visited Mother in her room, shed tears, and gave expressions of love through hugs and kisses. My siblings and I never forgot the words Dad and Mother told us: *I love you.* As they were leaving the room, they repeated the same words. *I love you.*

Caregivers, do not wait until death to shower your loved one with flowers and words of praise. He or she will not hear, see, or know. Why not let your loved one hear your words of praise and utterance of affection while living?

Be kind to me.
Be patient with me.
Be gentle to me.
Love me.

Talk to me.
Spend time with me.
Speak kind words to me.
Respect me.

Take care of me.
Read to me.

Pray with me.
Pray for me.

Manifest love to me.
Love me unconditionally.
Love me with all your heart.

Don't only tell me—
Show me.

Love never fails. (1 Corinthians 13:8 NIV)

Over time, it became arduous getting Mother in and out of my automobile. Going to the physician exhausted both of us. Her health continued to decline. I desired to stop the deterioration of her body and mind, but I could not. God was in control. I had to accept His will and ask Him to give me wisdom (James 1:5), strength (Isaiah 40:29), help (Psalm 46:1), and peace (Isaiah 26:3).

Caregivers, no matter what I was going through, I experienced an indescribable peace in God's presence. This was my place of rest. I concealed His Word in my heart (Psalm 119:11). Do you know why? The Holy Spirit brought the right Bible verse to my mind at the appropriate time. His Word soothed my discouraged heart. It strengthened my weary bones; it invigorated my body; it healed my broken heart; it brought comfort, joy, and peace to my soul.

Caregivers, the Bible is your guidebook. It has everything you need. Read and delight yourself in it at all times. On numerous occasions, when I was still before God, He brought to my mind a Bible verse to give me strength and encouragement. Communicating with God through prayer and reading His Word will help you to develop an intimate relationship with Him.

All you need, caregivers,
God will give you

When you pray in His name
According to His will.

Keep praying.
Keep reading the Word.

Keep trusting.
Keep giving thanks.

Stay in His presence.
Receive His peace.

In the midst of one of Lonnie Jr's visits to Chattanooga, he accompanied Mother and me to the primary care physician's (PCP) office for her annual examination. Before the PCP examined Mother, he observed me lifting her from the wheelchair. After the observation, he commented, "You need training." He made all the arrangements for home health services. Her team consisted of the following: social worker (SW), registered nurse (RN), certified nursing assistant (CNA), physical therapist (PT), and occupational therapist (OT).

> Caregivers, God answered my prayer by sending superior healthcare professionals to provide specific training. He is trustworthy. He is always on time. He provides in abundance.

Each healthcare professional played a major role in providing the best care for my beloved mother. I praised and acknowledged God. He alone deserved all the praise and honor.

Mother's first visit was with the social worker. She provided me with a list of transportation services I could use to transport Mother to her healthcare professionals. The transportation service I chose was not free, but Mother and I benefited from the privacy. She gave me advice and resources to guide me in making wise decisions about Mother's care.

The RN educated me about Mother's health. She coordinated with the PCP to create a care plan and to keep an eye on each and every aspect of Mother's physical wellness. She was calm, pleasant, inclusive, and meticulous.

I was privileged to have had a CNA who was compassionate, gentle, and cordial. She had immeasurable knowledge and taught and trained me. God sent her to me. She was patient, a remarkable encourager, and an unparalleled CNA.

The PT initiated a plan to keep Mother mobile as much as possible. First, she demonstrated what she wanted me to learn. Next, we practiced together. Then, the independent practice occurred. She was all-inclusive, conscientious, and congenial.

The OT obtained the medical equipment I needed to care for Mother. She made certain that I had the appropriate wheelchair and mattress for the bed. She was comprehensive, accommodating, and amicable.

God provided the training I needed through home health. He chose the right healthcare professionals just for me. All praise goes to Him. I cannot give Him enough adulation for what He did for me.

God will take care of me.
I am His child.

When I ask in His name
According to His will,
He will answer me.

I can trust Him.
He will deliver.
God will take care of me.

Caregivers, I participated in every aspect of Mother's care. I asked questions. When I required support, I knew I could call the doctor, nurse, and other staff members. I established a professional relationship with the healthcare professionals and an intimate relationship with the Lord Jesus Christ. I encourage you to get to know your loved one's healthcare professionals. Make sure they know who you are. Do not be afraid to ask questions. Your loved one's physician is significant in giving you the aid you need. Do not be passive. Be diligently engaged. You are your loved one's spokesperson. If you have not received Jesus as your Savior and Lord, the time is now. Don't miss your opportunity. Tomorrow is not promised.

Behold, now is the accepted time; behold, now is the day of salvation. (2 Corinthians 6:2 KJV)

As the months progressed, Mother began having complications swallowing liquids. I requested information from the gastroenterologist about her condition, and he recommended a swallowing test. Meanwhile, Wilhelminia and Margaret made several suggestions, but they were futile. Finally, Margaret stated, "Use a teaspoon." It worked. *Thank you, Lord*, I affirmed. Mother fed herself and swallowed food fine.

The next day, I sought information from Mother's PCP. He made arrangements for a speech therapist to visit her. During the visitation, a swallowing test was administered. She observed me using a teaspoon to dispense liquids to Mother and suggested I continue the method I was using; however, if I required further assistance to call the PCP.

Caregivers, sometimes I felt inadequate and was afraid I would make wrong decisions about Mother's care. I attempted to do everything perfectly, but I failed each time. When I tried in my own strength, I lost focus, strength, and peace, and my circumstances overwhelmed me. The Word assured me that the Lord's grace was enough for me, and His strength was perfect in my weakness (2 Corinthians 12:9). Try trusting Him in all your situations, circumstances, problems, and trials. No one can take care of you like Him; no one can give you peace like Him. Seek His will in all you do. I encourage you to take everything to Him in prayer. Then rest in His sufficiency, rest in His sovereignty, and relax in His everlasting arms as you wait on Him.

Trusting You,
O Lord.

Resting in
You.

3

Concluding Years

2013–2014

L eading up to 2013, Mother's care plan changed. Still, we appreciated and esteemed our precious moments together. Each morning God awakened her, she glanced around the room searching for me. When she saw my face, she smiled. I leaned forward so she could pat my face. Her gorgeous eyes and breathtaking smile captivated me. Her touch and eyes fixed on me were ardent. I prayed, hugged, kissed, and told her I loved her. She struggled to communicate with me verbally. From time to time, she called my name and murmured the words, "Thank you. I love you." Most times she articulated with her hands or eyes. Our sacred time together meant so much to me.

On a serene morning in 2013, the nurse arrived at my home. She greeted Mother and began examining her. During the examination, she asked me several questions. Then she recommended I give Mother's baths and personal care in the bed for safety precautions. I replied, "Bed baths? How am I going to do this well?" She assured me that the CNA would train and support me. As I sat in silence in the presence of the Lord and remembered His promises, I declared that there is nothing too hard for Him. I began praying some of His promises back to Him and claiming them.

The next day, the CNA arrived early at my home. She was prepared to teach and train me. During week 1, she demonstrated, and I watched her in a thorough manner. While giving instructions, she spoke to Mother and me in a soft, pleasant voice. During week 2, I took charge. She observed and made suggestions. Then she presented me with a care plan for my beloved mother. During week 3, she taught me how to shampoo Mother's hair in the bed. God blessed me with an outstanding teacher. She had excellent communication and listening skills.

I prayed, *Thank You, Lord, for helping me. There is no one like You—all-knowing One, all-powerful One.*

> Caregivers, stay close to the Lord. He is your focal point. Pray and keep trusting Him. You need Him more than anything and anyone else. Remember, He never fails to fulfill His promises. He is truth and cannot lie (Titus 1:2; Hebrews 6:18).

In your presence, Lord,
I must be.

In your presence,
Experiencing peace and joy.

At the beginning of 2014, caring for Mother was involved and complex. She had begun to cough while sleeping. I slept on the recliner in her room to monitor her and to be in close proximity. During the nurse's visit, I voiced my concerns about the coughing. As she demonstrated what I needed to do, I watched her with full attention and focus. Then I asked for repeated demonstrations. Why? I did not want to hurt my beloved mother.

One night while Mother was sleeping, she coughed time after time. It frightened me. *Help me, Jesus*, I thought. I followed the nurse's instructions. Afterward, I sat Mother in the wheelchair and moved it near the recliner where I slept. Then I held her hand, and we both fell asleep.

Before dawn, I massaged Mother's hands and feet, expressing my love. She kept her eyes on me closely, patting my face over and over again. When the nurse arrived that morning, I told her about the coughing experience. She examined Mother and suggested a soft-food diet. Again she demonstrated what I needed to do and accommodated me with meal planning.

Later in the year, the food Mother consumed caused her to cough from time to time. Before long, she began to cough often. She had an onerous time digesting and processing food. She had become frail, and her intake of food decreased. I called 911 for medical assistance. The emergency medical technicians (EMTs) transported Mother to the emergency room. After the completion of several tests, she was diagnosed with dysphagia, a swallowing disorder. The doctor on duty indicated that he had communicated information to the PCP and that we should follow up with him.

The next day, the nurse called to schedule a date and a time for the speech therapist to visit Mother. On the day of the visitation, she directed me to feed Mother while she carefully observed. She stated Mother held the food in her mouth, and I should consult the PCP about hospice. *Lord, help me*, I prayed. *Father, help me.* I wept. I called the gastroenterologist's office and communicated the problem to the nurse. She made an appointment at the hospital for a swallowing test. I felt weary. I ceased striving and became still before God. The Holy Spirit reminded me of God's promise at the commencement of my calling.

> Never will I leave you; never will I forsake you.
> (Hebrews 13:5 NIV)

Two days later, I proceeded with my daily routine. At Mother's breakfast feeding, she coughed and coughed. I considered she had an appointment scheduled for the swallowing test at the hospital. Nevertheless, I dialed 911 for transportation to the emergency room. The physician admitted her to the hospital. I was filled with gratitude. *Thank you, Lord*, I prayed.

> When all my strength is consumed,
> I look to You, Lord,
> For my strength comes from You.
>
> I look to You, Lord,
> For my help comes from You.

Physicians labored to rectify Mother's symptoms—abnormal sodium and swallowing disorder. The nurse notified me that a swallowing test would be administered. *Father, take away my anxieties and give me peace.* I prayed.

After the test, the hospitalist and nurse practitioner shared the results with me. The hospitalist alluded to the feeding tube as an option to correct the swallowing disorder. She indicated that the gastroenterologist would provide me with more detailed information. It was too much and too soon for me to make a swift decision. I waited until Mother's sodium stabilized.

In the course of time, Mother's sodium leveled. The hospitalist and nurse practitioner reminded me that a decision had to be made. I became impassioned. I knew Mother was frail. *Lord, help me.*

The next day, the gastroenterologist met with me. He explained the situation well and answered my questions in-depth. After the consultation, He stared at Mother's petite body and remarked, "You have taken care of her for so many years." *Nobody but the Lord*, I thought.

After the gastroenterologist left the room, I began to pace rapidly back and forth. My tears like raindrops streamed softly and uncontrollably down my cheeks. My husband patiently listened to me again and again as I expressed my emotional pain. He never spoke. My family gave me love and support.

That night at the hospital, I labored in prayer, crying out to the Lord and asking Him for wisdom and guidance. No one could understand my pain like Jesus; no one could give me the help I needed but Jesus. *Jesus! Jesus! Jesus!*

O sovereign LORD,
I hope in You,

Trusting You;
You know everything.

All-powerful One,
All-wise One,
All-knowing One,
Help me.

Take my worries and my anxieties.
I know You care for me.

I am weak; my strength is depleted.
Revive me.

I directed my attention to Mother's frail body. Then I asked myself the following questions: Was it worth it? Would it be a hindrance? Would there be complications? Was she weary?

What would she tell me to do? "Father, help me!" I cried. "In the all-knowing and all-wise name of Jesus, grant me peace."

God awakened me the next morning at the hospital with His supernatural peace. I cannot explain it. I prayed before calling my siblings to relay my answer to them: no feeding tube. They comforted me with gracious words.

> Gracious words are a honeycomb, sweet to the soul
> and healing to the bones. (Proverbs 16:24 NIV)

Later that morning, I communicated my decision to the hospitalist and nurse practitioner. During our conversation, they both encouraged me to use hospice for support. They made all the necessary arrangements for an interview to be held at the hospital the following day.

Before the meeting, I spent quiet time with the Lord. I asked the CNA to assist me with getting Mother out of the bed. I wanted her to be included and seated near me. Throughout the dialogue, we held hands the entire time. As the interviewer conversed with me, tears flowed from my eyes. It was an emotional day for me.

After the meeting, the nurse practitioner discussed with me the dismissal date for Mother. I thought about the availability of the doctors, nurses, and medical equipment she had in the hospital. *What am I going to do?* I asked the Lord.

> My grace is all you need. My power works best in
> weakness. (2 Corinthians 12:9 NLT)
>
> Do not fear, for I am with you; do not be afraid, for
> I am your God. I will strengthen you; I will help
> you; I will hold on to you with my righteous right
> hand. (Isaiah 41:10 CSB)

I will never leave you nor forsake you. (Hebrews 13:5 ESV)

On a Friday evening, a staff member told me Mother would be discharged from the hospital on Saturday. Soon after, a staff member from hospice called me at the hospital to inform me the commencing day for care was scheduled for Monday. I expressed to her that I needed assistance on the discharged day. She said I needed to voice my concerns to the administrative staff. I prayed. Then I imparted my thoughts and concerns to the nurse practitioner. He was in agreement. "Thank you, Lord," I whispered.

On December 29, 2014, the emergency medical technicians arrived at my resident from the hospital with my beloved mother. They sat her in the wheelchair and departed. Her eyes were open to the fullest. She stared at me with those beautiful eyes and smiled. She was delighted to be at home. I held her near to me, hugging and kissing her over and over again.

While I was talking to Mother, the doorbell rang. The nurse from hospice had arrived. She greeted Mother and introduced herself. I had several questions, but I waited for the assessment to be completed. She assisted me with Mother's bath. Then we had an informative conversation.

Hospice took control of Mother's care on December 29, 2014, her dismissal date. The hospice staff was there to support me during the final phase of her life on earth.

Caregivers, only God can give you inner peace. His peace is perfect. How do you receive inner peace? Keep your mind on Him and trust Him with all your heart.

You will show me the way of life,
granting me the joy of your presence
and the pleasures of living with you forever.
—Psalm 16:11 NLT

4

Homegoing

The physician from hospice gave me an estimation of Mother's time left on earth. *Why did she speak those words?* I wondered. I could not conceive my beloved mother was going to leave me. I exhausted myself trying to keep her alive. My sister, Wilhelminia, proclaimed, "Cal, let her go." I labored arduously to prevent Mother's soul from going home to be with the Lord. Why? I was egocentric, thinking only of myself.

> Caregivers, imagine me attempting to assist Elohim, the Creator God. I asked myself, *Carolyn, have you lost your mind?* I took my eyes off Him and experienced an emotional trauma. I confessed my sin and refocused, remaining in His presence, concentrating on His promises, and calling on His name. The hospice's physician gave me an estimation. Only God knew when. He is the Creator.

While lying in my beloved mother's bed close to her, I held her silky soft hand to my face. With tears flowing down my cheeks, I communicated to her my love again and again. I thanked her for being a blessing to me by her godly example. I held her near me—embracing her, kissing her, and caressing her face and hands over and over. God gave me the strength to tell her I was going to be okay. Then there was complete silence. I made an effort to give her a sip of water. She held her lips firmly. I ceased. I knew she was waiting on Him.

The Holy Spirit reminded me after Mother's death, her soul would pass into eternal life. Knowing her death would bring her swiftly into the presence of the Lord gave me an incomparable, satisfying peace and a deep joy in my heart. He comforted me with the following Bible verses.

> Absent from the body, and to be present with the Lord. (2 Corinthians 5:8 KJV)
>
> I am your God. I will strengthen you; I will help you. (Isaiah 41:10 CSB)
>
> The LORD is close to the brokenhearted. (Psalm 34:18 NIV)
>
> Precious in the sight of the LORD is the death of his saints. (Psalm 116:15 KJV)
>
> Blessed be God, even the Father of our Lord Jesus Christ, the Father of mercies, and the God of all comfort. (2 Corinthians 1:3 KJV)

Caregivers, it is comforting to know when believers fall asleep in Christ, they will transition from this life into eternal life. Jesus said, "I am the resurrection and the life. The one who believes in me, even if he dies, will live" (John 11:25 CSB). He is the only one who can give you the gifts of salvation and eternal life.

Thank You, Father, for the gifts of salvation and eternal life through Your Son, Jesus Christ—the only impeccable, all-sufficient sacrifice for sin.

My stunning mother at eighty-one years old in Chattanooga, Tennessee, at a brunch.

Soon, praise the Lord,
I am going to see
My Savior, Jesus Christ.

Praise the Lord,
Praise the Lord,
I will see Him face-to-face.

Death is not the end, believers.
It is the beginning—
Eternity with the Lord.

Praise the Lord,
Praise the Lord.
I will see Him face-to-face.

God determined the perfect time to take Mother home to heaven. There is no one like Him, the Creator of heaven and Earth. Everything belongs to Him.

Mother closed her eyes, and her body fell asleep on January 13, 2015. Her soul was immediately in the presence of the Lord (2 Corinthians 5:8). What a glorious, joyful day that must have been when she opened her eyes in heaven and saw her Savior and Lord face-to-face!

My gorgeous mother, at eighty-five years old, in Chattanooga, Tennessee, at a celebration dinner.

Face-to-face with Jesus Christ, my Savior,
My sinless substitute.

He shed His blood
And died on the cross for me.

He rose again
To give me life eternally.

Face-to-face with my Redeemer,
In His presence forevermore.

A beautiful photo of Mother in her twenties, in LaGrange, Georgia.

In the third heaven
Where He dwells,
I am here
With all the saints.

The Savior is here.
Believe in Him
And live forevermore.

When you get to heaven, saints
Oh! Oh! Oh! What a day of rejoicing that will be
When you see Jesus, your Savior and Lord
You'll sing and shout the victory
—Adapted from "When We All Get to Heaven" by
Eliza E. Hewitt and Emily D. Wilson

Mother transitioned into eternal life on January 13, 2015, at age eighty-nine. Mother's soul was set free, delivered from her mortal body. All those imperfect parts that afflicted her earthly body and mind vanished. All of life's cares disappeared. Her life on Earth climaxed. She was ready. Are you ready?

Caregivers, heaven is a real place. There is only one way to this place—through Jesus Christ alone (John 14:6). "Neither is there salvation in any other: for there is none other name under heaven given among men, whereby we must be saved" (Acts 4:12 KJV). Death is excruciating; however, believers can be confident that beyond the grave is hope through Jesus Christ our Lord (1 Corinthians 15:50–55).

Thank God! He gives us victory over sin and death through our Lord Jesus Christ. (1 Corinthians 15:57 NLT)

Whatever you do, do your work heartily, as for the Lord and not for people, knowing that it is from the Lord that you will receive the reward of the inheritance. It is the Lord Christ whom you serve.
—Colossians 3:23–24 NASB

5

Homegoing Anniversary

Mother's soul departed this earth January 13, 2015. A year later, January 13, 2016, I missed her so much.

I miss you, my beloved mother.
By writing, I am healing.
By God's grace, I am moving forward.

I laugh,
I cry,

And I remember all the marvelous times we shared.
I am jubilant you are in heaven,
Experiencing ecstatic joy.

Your memories are a blessing
And will last until I see your lovely face again.

As I sat in my bedroom early morning on January 13, 2016, I remembered the precious moments Mother and I shared together. Tears flowed down my cheeks. I used my hand and began patting my face the way she did, repeating the words, *I love you. I miss you.* She was an amazing woman.

A woman who
Revered the Lord.

A woman whose

Conversation and conduct
Were in agreement with another.

A woman who
showed and demonstrated
Her love.

A woman who
Had a powerful impact
On my life.

A saved woman whose
Destination is
Heaven.

A godly woman who
Will be profoundly
Missed by me.

I do not know what you want me to do, I said to God. I prayed and prayed. Then in silence, I waited. And waited. On Mother's first anniversary in heaven—January 13, 2016—the Holy Spirit revealed to me the good news through Gospel tracts. The Gospel is the good news that Christ died for our sins. He was buried. He was raised from the dead on the third day (1 Corinthians 15:3–4). What a wonderful way to celebrate my beloved mother's anniversary! I pondered, *How do I proceed with such an awesome calling?* I did not know the answers to the when, where, and how. I prayed and petitioned God for wisdom, and I trusted Him.

On a frigid, sunny day later that January, I embarked on another calling: sharing the Gospel in the mall. I commenced by leaving tracts in the seating areas. After two weeks, I became disgruntled with using this method only. I desired to interact with the shoppers. I asked the Lord for courage and power.

The following week, I reached out to the shoppers with Gospel tracts. The Holy Spirit empowered me, and He made me courageous. *Thank you, Lord,* I prayed. I was greeted with smiles, thank-yous, and rejections. Regardless of the denials, I had a feeling of great joy and triumph. For those individuals who repudiated the message, I prayed for them and kept moving.

Sharing the good news in the mall ceased in September 2016. The general manager informed me the mall was private property and that distributing tracts was not allowed. He added that he did not refute the message. After he finished speaking, I ministered to Him with a tract. I felt somber but appreciative to God for the opportunity, experience, and eight months to share the good news in the mall. Trusting God was vastly superior to my human understanding. Giving up was not an option. God called me. He was not going to turn His back on me. I telephoned a tract ministry and requested information. After reading the data, I was surprised, encouraged, and motivated. My personal ministry came into full fruition in December 2016 as I continued sharing the good news through Gospel tracts. I disseminated tracts to assisted living facilities, nursing homes, individuals, churches, shelters, a detention facility, and a jail. I distributed Bibles and gifts for Christmas to some of these facilities. Two nursing homes received a complete Bible on CD. I am trusting God to provide financially for this ministry. He makes the impossible achievable.

> Therefore, my dear brothers and sisters, stand firm. Let nothing move you. Always give yourselves fully to the work of the Lord, because you know that your labor in the Lord is not in vain. (1 Corinthians 15:58 NIV)

6

Caregiving

G OD CALLED A SPECIAL PERSON like you to be a caregiver. You love unselfishly, expecting nothing in return. You exemplify God's love because of His great love for you. You love with complete sincerity and commitment. You are steadfast, empathetic, attentive, trustworthy, patient, and dependable.

You are one of a kind,
Created by God.

You are gentle,
Yet you are strong.

Your love is shown
Through Jesus Christ alone.

You are beautiful. Peerless. Resilient. Extraordinary.
You are the caregiver
Called by God.

My closing statements to you, caregivers:

- Trials, circumstances, suffering, pain, and death can make it extremely challenging for you to see God's purpose. Often we forget that He is working all things for our good (Romans 8:28). Always remember He called you to be a caregiver for a purpose. Trust Him. Talk to Him about everything. From time to time, your circumstances may be unbearable. Do not give up. Instead, keep praying, keep trusting, keep your eyes focused on Him, and give all your worries and anxieties to Him. Do you know who He is? He is sovereign. He controls your circumstances.

- If you feel like you need to complain, go to God first. Attempt to replace complaining with thanksgiving. Do not look for any earthly accolades for this calling; however, look for eternal rewards. God sees all you do— He is El Roi. He knows all you do—He is omniscient.

- It is important for you to respect the rights of your loved one. Always include the care receiver in the decision-making process, unless there are mental disabilities. Express and show your love.

- When changes are made, there are adjustments. It affects you, the caregiver, and also the care receiver. Be patient.

- Pray: "Pray without ceasing" (1 Thessalonians 5:17 NASB)

- Trust: "Trust in the LORD with all your heart" (Proverbs 3:5 NIV).

- Thank: "In everything give thanks" (1 Thessalonians 5:18 NKJV).

- Laugh: "A cheerful heart is good medicine" (Proverbs 17:22 NLT).

- Read God's Word; study, mediate, memorize, and apply it (2 Timothy 2:15).

- Look to God, not your circumstances. If you cease looking to Him, you will experience anxiety, worry, fear, weakness, frustration, nervousness, complaining, and self-pity. Then you will plummet into a state of depression. Keep your eyes on Him.

- Review your loved one's healthcare coverage carefully. Mother spent several days in the hospital. Thanks be to God, her expenses were paid in full. Cheap coverage is not always the best. Adequate coverage is important.

- Occasionally, I think about the stress I received from not having an advance directive for Mother. I did not think to ask her about the quality of her life and treatments. Without an advance directive, all the decisions will be made by you, the caregiver. It can be overpowering and emotional. Most often, no one wants to discuss the death of a loved one. However, it is necessary. Do not procrastinate.

- Network with other caregivers, friends, or family members who will give you godly advice. You do not need any drama.

- Take care of your mental and physical health. Do not miss doctor appointments. Try to exercise, eat three meals a day, and rest. Attempt to take a vacation.

- Be vigilant for signs of depression. If needed, seek professional help immediately. Do not wait.

- Consult your loved one's physicians for resources and assistance. Develop a professional relationship with them. Do not be afraid to ask questions.

- Educate yourself about hospice. It is a magnificent nurturance.

- Use the resources provided by AARP Family Caregiving, included in this book.

- Do not blame yourself. Stop the "If I had ..." You did the best you knew how. Negative thoughts have no use or purpose.

- If you have believed and received Jesus Christ as your Savior and Lord, the Holy Spirit lives in you. He gives you power (Acts 1:8). He gives you inexhaustible or limitless guidance, help, comfort, strength, and peace. He is with you at all times—nonstop, forever (John 14:16–17).

- "Whatever you do, do it from the heart, as something done for the Lord and not for people" (Colossians 3:23 CSB).

- "I pray that God, the source of hope, will fill you completely with joy and peace because you trust him. Then you will overflow with confident hope through the power of the Holy Spirit" (Romans 15:13 NLT).

- "Now may the Lord of peace himself give you peace at all times in every way. The Lord be with you all" (2 Thessalonians 3:16 ESV).

It is of the LORD's mercies that we are not consumed, because his compassions fail not. They are new every morning: great is thy faithfulness.
—Lamentations 3:22–23 (KJV)

7

~~∿∽o੦೨⊶Ꙩ⊷੨ᴏ∿~~

Reflections

Reflecting on eleven years of caregiving and thinking passionately about how God brought me through bring tears to my eyes and jubilation to my soul. I had to trust Him to accomplish for me what I could never do in my own strength. He faithfully provided for me, protected me, loved me, and cared for me. How would I have made it without Him? *Unthinkable. Inconceivable. Unimaginable.* I remained in my calling without complaining because of Him. Otherwise, it would have been impossible. He gave me the staying power. He kept Mother in my care until He called her home to heaven. I found contentment in my calling because my sufficiency was in Him alone.

> You never left me—my JEHOVAH Immeka
> You were my peace—my JEHOVAH Shalom
> You were my strength—my JEHOVAH Uzzi
> You were my provider—my JEHOVAH Jireh
> You were my shepherd—my JEHOVAH Rohi
> You were my light—my JEHOVAH Ori
> You were my healer—my JEHOVAH Rapha
> You were faithful—my El Emunah

I recall how astonishing it was when God communicated with me through His powerful Word. Through prayer, I talked to Him; through His Word, He spoke to me. What an awe-inspiring experience—the intimacy, closeness, and fellowship I had with my Heavenly Father! My Father never lies. He never changes. He never fails to fulfill His promises. He will never leave or forsake me. He can be trusted. He awakened me early in the mornings to spend sacred time with Him. When my mornings were consumed, I repeated brief sentences to Him in the name of Jesus. I memorized Bible verses and recited them. It was necessary for me to spend quality time alone with Him. During those precious times, the intimacy of our relationship grew.

Here are a few brief sentences I stated time and again to God.

- I need You.
- Help me.
- I am helpless without You.
- I trust You.
- I praise You.
- Strengthen me.
- Equip me for this day.
- Take control of my life.
- Give me rest.
- I love You.
- Help me not to complain.
- Lead me.
- Help my light to shine.
- Forgive me.
- Thank You.
- Empower me.
- Have mercy on me.
- Give me peace.
- Take care of me.
- Guide me through this day.
- Help me to make wise decisions.
- Help me to pray about everything.
- Give me wisdom and knowledge.
- Help me to live one day at a time.
- I cannot do anything without You.
- Help me to glorify You in all that I think, say, and do.
- Teach me how to be a caregiver.

- Jesus, Jesus, Jesus.
- Jesus, help me.

As I look back, I realize the demise of my beloved mother was heartbreaking. I had a difficult time letting her go. *What am I going to do?* I thought. I, I, I—it was all about me. At that moment, I did not think about her destination—heaven in the presence of her Savior and Lord. Her death was painful, but it had no power over her (Romans 8:11; 1 Corinthians 15:54–57). *I will see you again, my beloved.*

Almighty God had a specific plan and special purpose for my life, even before I was created. He miraculously planned for me to achieve something amazing for His kingdom through caregiving. In my trials, circumstances, sufferings, problems, or difficulties, He is making me more and more like Christ. Through His plan, He is using all things to accomplish His purpose. Therefore, I know He called me to be a caregiver "for such a time as this" (Esther 4:14).

> For such a time as this
> I was placed upon the earth
> To hear the voice of God
> And do His will …
> For such a time as this.
> —Wayne Watson, "For Such a Time as This"

May he equip you with all you need for doing his will. May he produce in you, through the power of Jesus Christ, every good thing that is pleasing to him. All glory to him forever and ever! Amen. (Hebrews 13:21 NLT)

Part Two

ENCOURAGING BIBLE VERSES

Study to shew thyself approved unto God, a workman that needeth not to be ashamed, rightly dividing the word of truth.
—2 Timothy 2:15 (KJV)

Read them.
Study them.
Meditate on them.
Memorize them.
Apply them.

Practice! Practice! Practice!

1 Trusting in the LORD

Trust in the LORD with all thine heart; and lean
not unto thine own understanding. In all thy ways
acknowledge him, and he shall direct thy paths.
—Proverbs 3:5–6 (KJV)

King Solomon gave wise instruction and a powerful promise to his son. Pay attention to the word *all* he used in verses 5 and 6. He utilized three commands—trust, lean not, and acknowledge. What will happen if you follow and obey the instruction given by King Solomon? The Lord will show you which path to take (Proverbs 3:6).

A Personal Note from the Author

The Holy Spirit reminds me, through the Word, I am to trust in the Lord with all my heart. Why? He is trustworthy. I pray often, asking Him to help me when I do not know the answers or details right away in my situation and to help me obey and trust Him when I do not comprehend why. I must trust and acknowledge the One who is the sovereign, infinite, all-knowledge, all-powerful, all-present, all-wise, reliable, faithful, immutable Creator. He never lies and never makes mistakes.

My human understanding always gets me into trouble. I cannot trust myself. I am limited, and I am not God. It is vital for me to hide His Word in my heart. It is through His Word I can assertively claim my trust in Him. My limited knowledge leads to frustration, stress, worrying, and anxiety. For that reason, I must live my life by obeying the Lord, trusting in His sovereignty, trusting in His promises, and acknowledging Him in all that I do.

Encouraging Bible Verses

James 4:13–15

Psalm 62:8

Psalm 56:3

Psalm 37:5

Psalm 84:12

1 Corinthians 13:12

Notes

2 Are You Worried or Anxious?

Don't worry about anything; instead, pray about everything.
Tell God what you need, and thank him for all he has done.
　　　　　　　—Philippians 4:6 (NLT)

According to Philippians 4:6, believers are to dismiss worrying and pray. Paul gives a command and a solution in Philippians 4:6. In Philippians 4:7, he gives a promise.

> Command: Don't worry about anything.
> Solution: Pray about everything; pray with
> thanksgiving.
> Promise: Peace (Philippians 4:7).

If you follow Paul's command and solution, you will receive the peace of God "which surpasses all human understanding" (Philippians 4:7).

A Personal Note from the Author

Daily, the Holy Spirit reminds me, through God's Word, worrying and anxiety are futile. I am under persistent attack by Satan. I must dress myself for the battle with the Armor of God, my protective clothing (Ephesians 6:10–18). The Bible teaches me my struggle is not against flesh and blood but against the rulers, against the authorities, against the cosmic powers of this darkness, against evil, and against spiritual forces in the heavens (Ephesians 6:11–17). His main purpose is to steal, kill, and destroy me (John 10:10a). When he attacks me, I must use my spiritual weapons—prayer and the Word. These powerful weapons protect me from worrying and anxiety. I cannot fight

Satan in my own strength; he is too strong for me. As a result, I must live my life by praying, by filling my mind with the Word of God, by relying on God's strength, by trusting Him with all my heart to fight for me, by dressing myself for the battle, and by thanking Him for all he has done.

Worrying and anxiety steal my joy
And deprive my peace.

Prayer and the Word of God
Bring joy and peace to my fatigued soul.

Encouraging Bible Verses

Matthew 6:25–34

1 Peter 5:7

Psalm 55:22

Notes

3 Why Fear?

Do not fear, for I am with you.
—Isaiah 41:10 (CSB)

The Lord commanded Israel not to fear. Why? He promised, "I am with you." These are consoling and encouraging words spoken by the Lord Himself.

Command: Do not fear.
Promise: I am with you.

No matter how difficult your situation or circumstance may be, He is there with you. You can trust Him. Ponder on these uplifting and comforting words: "I will never leave you nor forsake you" (Hebrews 13:5b).

A Personal Note from the Author

Fear is a joy stealer orchestrated by Satan. He attacks me relentlessly. He tries to take hold of my joy, my peace, my testimony, my faith, and my health. It is crucial for me to memorize Bible verses. Why? Because I know Satan will attack me again and again. When I am challenged by Him, the Holy Spirit brings Bible verses to my remembrance. I recite my verses out loud, repeating them over and over again. I use my other spiritual weapon, prayer, and I use the shield of faith (Ephesians 6:16).

There will be times when circumstances may cause me to fear, but I must recall that the Lord said, "Do not fear." He will always be there to strengthen me and to assist me. I do not have to fear. Why? I belong to Him. He has not given me a spirit of fear but of power, love, and a sound mind (2 Timothy 1:7). He will empower me with all that I need for life. I must remember to trust Him—not fear.

Encouraging Bible Verses

Isaiah 41:13

Joshua 1:9

Psalm 56:3

1 John 4:18

James 4:7

Isaiah 12:2

Notes

4 Confidence in Prayer

This is the confidence we have before him: If we ask
anything according to his will, he hears us.
—1 John 5:14 (CSB)

Ask God.
Ask anything according to His will.
Assurance: He hears you.

God answers your prayers according to His will. For that reason, your prayers must be conjoined or aligned with His will. The assurance you have is when your prayers are interconnected with His will, He hears you.

A Personal Note from the Author

During my sacred times alone with the Lord, He gives me strength, encouragement, peace, wisdom, rest, and power. Try escaping into the presence of the Lord in the stillness of the morning. Do not be so anxious to speak. Be still. Be quiet. Listen. Rest. Enjoy your intimate fellowship with Him. It is an awesome experience.

> I enjoy staring out of the window gazing at the breathtaking sceneries in the day sky and the night sky; peering at the spectacular sunrise and sunset; looking closely at the beauty of the sun and clouds; peering at the radiance of the moon and stars; capturing God's magnificent glory—worshipping, praising, thanking, and glorifying His name (Psalm 19:1–2).

In the Lord's presence, He fills me with inexpressible joy and a peace I cannot explain. This revered time spent alone with Him is my resting place. My relationship with Him is powerful.

> Be exhorted to pray at all times (1 Thessalonians 5:17).

> Pray with confidence (1 John 5:14).

> Pray according to His will, aligning your will with His will (1 John 5:14).

> Pray knowing that He will answer you, according to His will (1 John 5:14).

> Pray in His name (John 14:14).

> Come before Him with boldness (Hebrews 4:16).

Encouraging Bible Verses

Matthew 7:7

Colossians 4:2

Luke 18:1

Notes

5 Meditating on the Word

Keep this Book of the Law always on your lips; meditate on it day and night, so that you may be careful to do everything written in it. Then you will be prosperous and successful.
—Joshua 1:8 (NIV)

This Book of the Law in Joshua 1:8 is referring to the Torah, the first five books of the Hebrew Bible (Genesis, Exodus, Leviticus, Numbers, Deuteronomy). These books were written by Moses and later translated into Greek (Pentateuch).

The complete Bible consists of sixty-six books. It is divided into two parts, the Old Testament and the New Testament.

> All Scripture is given by inspiration of God, and is profitable for doctrine, for reproof, for correction, for instruction in righteousness, that the man of God may be complete, thoroughly equipped for every good work. (2 Timothy 3:16–17 NKJV)

Hide the Word in your heart. Fill your mind with it—reading, marking, highlighting, memorizing, speaking, writing, listening, and applying. You must not only read the Word but also meditate on it. Joshua said, "Meditate on it day and night." Ponder: think about it, study, recite, examine, review, reflect, and ask yourself questions. Always look to the Lord for His plan and His purpose for your life. Acknowledge Him in all areas of your life. Center your attention on permanent spiritual wealth, not the temporary wealth of this world. "Then you will be prosperous and successful." You must read, meditate, obey, and live the Word of God.

A Personal Note from the Author

Imagine my life without the Bible—terrifying! I cannot conceive living without the Word of God. Reading, meditating, obeying, and living the Word of God give me spiritual discernment, spiritual maturity, spiritual prosperity, and genuine success.

Encouraging Bible Verses

Psalm 1:2

Psalm 119:105

Psalm 119:11

2 Timothy 2:15

Notes

6 Waiting on the Lord

Wait on the LORD: be of good courage, and he shall
strengthen thine heart: wait, I say, on the LORD.
—Psalm 27:14 (KJV)

King David gives a command as well as a promise in Psalm
27:14. He states the command at the beginning of the verse.
Then he repeats it at the conclusion of the verse. He admonishes
you to wait on the Lord and take courage. In doing so, you have
been promised renewed strength.

Wait, I say, on the LORD. (Psalm 27:14 KJV)

A Personal Note from the Author

It is necessary for me to wait on the Lord's perfect timing to
bring about His desired will, purpose, and plan for my life.
He is teaching me to wait by seeking and depending on Him;
devoting myself to prayer and His Word; thanking and praising
Him; resting in His promises; acknowledging His sovereignty;
speaking to myself in "psalms, hymns, and spiritual songs"
(Ephesians 5:19). I must let go of all unnecessary worrying as
I wait patiently on Him. It is not easy waiting. That is why I
have to trust and depend on His strength. When I am without
strength, only He can rejuvenate my weary soul. I have to wait
expectantly knowing that He will answer me in His perfect
timing, according to His perfect will.

Yes, my soul, find rest in God;
my hope comes from him. (Psalm 62:5 NIV)

Encouraging Bible Verses

Isaiah 64:4

Isaiah 40:31

Psalm 37:7

Lamentations 3:25

Notes

7 Strength in Weakness

My grace is sufficient for you, for My strength
is made perfect in weakness.
—2 Corinthians 12:9 (NKJV)

Apostle Paul repeatedly petitioned the Lord to have the thorn in his flesh removed. The Lord responded with these comforting words: "My grace is sufficient for you. My strength is made perfect in weakness" (2 Corinthians 12:9). The essence of Paul's thorn is not known.

Paul's prayers were answered according to the Lord's will. He did not remove the thorn in Paul's flesh, but He gave him grace and strength to endure. His grace was sufficient to provide for what Paul needed in his weaknesses, sufferings, persecutions, and hardships. At the conclusion of 2 Corinthians 12:9 (NLT), Paul states, "So now I am glad to boast about my weaknesses, so that the power of Christ can work through me." In 2 Corinthians 12:10 (NLT), Paul says, "That's why I take pleasure in my weaknesses and in the insults, hardships, persecutions, and troubles that I suffer for Christ. For when I am weak, then I am strong."

A Personal Note from the Author

My weaknesses humble me.
My weaknesses draw me closer to the Lord.
My weaknesses renew my mind through the
Word.
My weaknesses keep me on my knees praying.

My weaknesses encourage me to trust in the
    Lord.

My weaknesses make me depend or rely on the
    Lord.

My weaknesses demonstrate the Lord's
    strength.

It is the Lord who gives me strength in my sufferings, hardships, circumstances, trials, or difficulties. I cannot do anything in my own strength. He is my source. Without Him, I am helpless. I need His supernatural strength. No matter what I am facing or will have to face in this life, I am confident the Lord's grace is sufficient for me, and His strength is made perfect in my weaknesses (2 Corinthians 12:9). He is my never-ending strength. With Him, I am able to endure my weaknesses.

Encouraging Bible Verses

Isaiah 40:29

Philippians 4:13

Isaiah 26:4

John 15:5

Notes

8 Peace in the Midst of a Trial

You keep him in perfect peace whose mind is
stayed on you, because he trusts in you.
—Isaiah 26:3 (ESV)

I f you keep your mind on the Lord and trust Him, you will be kept in perfect peace. He is your source and the only one who can give you perfect peace in the midst of a trial.

A Personal Note from the Author

When my mind remains on my trials, I have no peace. Stress attacks my mind and body. This attack comes from Satan. He will try anything to keep my mind off the Lord. However, when I trust the Lord, my mind is focused on Him. As a result, He offers me perfect peace. I run to Him and rest in His faithfulness, His promises, and His sovereignty. I know He is the only one who can give me perfect peace in the midst of my trials. He is my source—my only source.

Encouraging Bible Verses

John 16:33

John 14:27

Philippians 4:7

Psalm 4:8

Romans 5:1

Notes

9 Joy in the Midst of a Trial

Consider it all joy, my brothers and sisters,
when you encounter various trials.
—James 1:2 (NASB)

Apostle James gives a command in his letter to believers: "Consider it all joy." He does not say "consider it joy," but *all joy*. According to James 1:2, you cannot avoid trials; they are inescapable. Notice the word *when* not *if.* He is conveying to you that you are going to encounter various trials. Because they are certain to happen, try to evaluate or assess the manner by which you view or think about them—from your prospective or from God's prospective.

How can you count it all joy in the midst of a trial? Read James 1:3–4 to find your answer. After reading the verses, you should conclude it is all about your faith—trusting God in your trials. Apostle James states that trials test your faith and produce endurance. Each time you encounter a trial and choose to trust God, your faith matures.

> More trials
> More trust
> More maturity

> Trusting God
> Not the trial
> Reason to rejoice

A Personal Note from the Author

Trials are inevitable. I cannot escape them. Sometimes, they are exceedingly challenging and painful. However, I realize they serve a purpose. On numerous occasions, God uses my trials to strengthen my faith and grow my spiritual maturity. By studying the encouraging Bible verses, I know my trials produce endurance, develop my character, and conform me into the likeness of God's Son. No matter what trials I have to face in this life, I am assured that I will live with the Lord forever. My future is secured, protected, and safe. Paul wrote in Romans 8:18 (CSB), "For I consider the sufferings of this present time are not worth comparing with the glory that is going to be revealed to us." What a reason to rejoice!

Encouraging Bible Verses

Romans 5:3–4

Romans 8:18

1 Peter 1:6–7

2 Corinthians 4:17

2 Corinthians 4:18

Philippians 4:4

Notes

10 Death of a Believer

Absent from the body, and to be present with the Lord.
—2 Corinthians 5:8 (KJV)

What Happens to a Believer after Death?

Mother's body fell asleep—not her soul. Her soul does not sleep. Her body was buried in the ground. What about her soul? Her soul was removed at the time of physical death (Genesis 35:18; Ecclesiastes 12:7). After her death, her soul was immediately escorted into the presence of the Lord. Apostle Paul expresses this perspective in 2 Corinthians 5:8 (KJV), "Absent from the body, and to be present with the Lord." Where is the Lord? He is in heaven. Heaven is where He lives (Matthew 5:16; 6:9; John 14:2).

What does it mean to be absent from the body and to be present with the Lord? It means death. Death is a separation of body and soul.

After Mother's death, her soul was separated from her body and carried instantly into the presence of the Lord. Her body sleeps in the grave. Likewise, the soul of each individual who has accepted Jesus Christ as Savior and Lord will be taken immediately into the presence of the Lord, after death.

The Church-age believers can look forward to the Lord's return (rapture) with the souls of believers who have fallen asleep in Him. At this event, the Lord will descend from heaven with a shout, with the voice of the archangel, and with the trumpet of God. The deceased, physical body will be resurrected first in a transformed, glorified, eternal body and reunited with the soul. What will happen to those believers who are still living? Their bodies will be changed and will be caught up together with them in the clouds to meet the Lord in the air (1 Thessalonians 4:13–17; 1 Corinthians 15:50–54).

Note: This is a temporary location (heaven) for Church-age believers. The rapture takes place in the air—not on earth. This is a separate event from the Second Coming of the Lord to the Earth.

At the rapture, believers (deceased and alive) will be taken up into heaven. Two events will take place: the Judgment Seat of Christ (2 Corinthians 5:10; Romans 14:10–12; 1 Corinthians 3:10–15) and the Marriage Supper of the Lamb (Revelation 19:7–9). The Marriage Supper of the Lamb will take place before the Second Coming of Christ.

However, this is not the conclusion for the Church-age believers. Succeeding the Judgment Seat of Christ and the Marriage Supper of the Lamb is the Second Coming of Christ (Revelation 1:7; Matthew 24:29–31; Revelation 19:11–21). As you continue reading and studying Revelation, you will encounter the next event, the Thousand-Year Reign of Christ, the Millennium (Revelation 20:1–4). Finally, your second location will be revealed (Revelation 21, 22). Where is your second location?

Note: The tribulation is not mentioned because the Church-age believers will be in heaven with the Lord. The tribulation will be for unbelievers. However, there will be souls saved during the tribulation (Revelation 7:9–14). Praise the Lord.

I challenge you to search the Bible to discover what will happen to unbelievers when they die and their final destination.

Encouraging Bible Verses

Philippians 1:21–23

Acts 7:59

Luke 16:19–31

Notes

11 Why Do You Need a Savior?

When Adam sinned, sin entered the world.
Adam's sin brought death, so death spread
to everyone, for everyone sinned.
—Romans 5:12 (NLT)

S in entered the world by one man—Adam. God commanded Adam that he could eat of every tree in the garden with the exception of the knowledge of good and evil. God made His command plain to him and defined the consequences clearly for disobedience, "You will surely die" (Genesis 2:16–17). Notice God did not tell Adam he would die, but he would "surely die."

In spite of what God told Adam, he still disobeyed His command and died spiritually. The fellowship no longer existed among God, Adam, and Eve. Why? Sin separated them from a holy God (Isaiah 59:2). However, God continued to communicate and provide for them. He made garments of skin for them as a covering by sacrificing an animal (Genesis 3:21). God also imposed sentences on Adam and Eve (Genesis 3:16–17, 22–24). In the course of time, they died a physical death—all because of sin. Sin has devastating consequences. It always leads to death. There is no forgiveness of sin without the shedding of blood (Hebrews 9:22). Remember, God sacrificed an animal to cover Adam and Eve's sin. Blood was shed, and an animal died.

The sin nature of Adam passed on to you, because of his sin (Romans 5:12). After you were created in your mother's womb, you were conceived as a sinner (Psalm 51:5.) As a result, you were born a sinner spiritually separated from a holy God (Isaiah 59:2) and destined to die (Romans 6:23a).

God made Christ, who never sinned, to be the offering for our sin, so that we could be made right with God through Christ. (2 Corinthians 5:21 NLT)

Why do you need a Savior? You need a Savior because you are a sinner (Romans 3:23).

For as in Adam all die, even so in Christ shall all be made alive. (1 Corinthians 15:22 KJV)

Encouraging Bible Verses

John 3:17–18

Romans 8:1

Notes

12 What Is the Gospel Message?

Christ died for our sins according to the Scriptures,
that he was buried, that he was raised on the
third day according to the Scriptures.
—1 Corinthians 15:3–4 (CSB)

The Gospel message is the good news that Christ died for your sin. He was buried, and He was raised from the dead.

Truth #1: Christ Died for Your Sin

Why did Christ die? He died to pay the penalty for your sin. Before the creation of the world, God had a marvelous plan to redeem you through the blood of His Son, Jesus Christ (Ephesians 1:4; Colossians 1:14). Because of His great love for you, He gave His Son to die for your sin (John 3:16; Romans 5:8). Only He could atone for your sin. Why? He is the only One without sin.

On the cross, an amazing thing transpired. God made Christ to be sin for you—who never sinned—so that in Christ you could be made right with Him (2 Corinthians 5:21). Your sin debt was paid in full by the shed blood of Jesus Christ. His blood made peace with God (Colossians 1:20). The death of Jesus was confirmed at the cross (John 19:31–37). His death was prophesied in Isaiah 53.

Do you believe that Christ died for your sin?

Truth #2: He Was Buried

The burial of Christ is a crucial truth of the Gospel message. If He had not been buried, there would be no resurrection. His burial was real.

The following Bible verses provide proof that Christ was buried:

- Paul stated in 1 Corinthians 15:4 that Christ was buried.
- Jesus Himself referred to His burial in Matthew 12:40.
- Joseph of Arimathea and Nicodemus prepared the body of Jesus for burial and buried Him in a tomb (John 19:38–42).
- His burial was prophesied in Isaiah 53.

If you deny this truth—burial of Christ—it is impossible for you to believe the Gospel message.

Do you believe that Christ was buried?

Truth #3: He Was Raised on the Third Day

The third truth of the Gospel message is the resurrection of Jesus Christ from the dead. If He had remained in the grave, you would be still in your sin; your faith would be useless; you would have no hope—no Savior, no forgiveness, no salvation, no Holy Spirit, and no eternal life. Jesus declared that He would rise three days after His death (Matthew 16:21; Matthew 17:23; Matthew 20:19).

Listed below are appearances of Jesus after His resurrection:

- Mary Magdalene (John 20:11–17)
- Other women (Matthew 28:5–7; Matthew 28:9–10)
- Two on the road to Emmaus (Luke 24:13–32)
- Simon Peter (Luke 24:33–35)

- Disciples without Thomas (John 20:19–24)
- Disciples with Thomas (John 20:26–31)

Paul gave numerous post-resurrection appearances of Jesus Christ in 1 Corinthians 15:5–8).

- He appeared to Cephas (Peter).
- He was seen by the twelve.
- He appeared to more than five hundred of His followers at one time.
- He appeared to His half-brother, Apostle James.
- He appeared to all the apostles.
- He appeared to Apostle Paul.

Do you believe that Christ was raised from the grave? Do you believe the Gospel message?

Will you think earnestly about God's great love for you? He loved you so much. He shed His blood and died on the cross for your sin (John 3:16; Romans 5:8; Hebrews 9:22b). He offers you the gifts of salvation and eternal life through His only Son, Jesus Christ.

Where is your eternal destination? There are only two choices— heaven or hell. It is your choice.

If you have not received Jesus Christ as your Savior and Lord, will you:

Admit that you a sinner (Romans 3:23)?

Repent be willing to turn from your sin and turn to God through Jesus Christ (Luke 13:5; Mark 1:15)?

Believe the Gospel? The Gospel is the good news that Jesus Christ died for your sin, was buried, and was raised on the third day (1 Corinthians 15:3-4).

Through prayer, will you invite Jesus Christ to come into your heart and save you? Will you **confess** and **receive** Him as your Savior and Lord (Romans 10:9; John 1:12)?

Here is a prayer to recite.

> Dear God,
>
> I am a sinner and need a Savior. I am willing to turn from my sin and turn to You through Jesus Christ. I believe that Christ died for my sin. He was buried, and He rose from the grave on the third day. Come into my heart, Jesus, and save me. I confess and receive You as my Savior and Lord. In the saving name of Jesus, amen.

In this prayer, you are relying on God for forgiveness and salvation.

Remember,
Admit,
Repent,
Believe,
Confess and Receive.

Encouraging Bible Verses

John 3:16

Romans 3:23

Romans 3:10

Romans 5:8

Romans 6:23

Mark 1:15

Acts 3:19

Acts 20:21

Romans 5:8

Roman 10:9

Romans 10:13

Ephesians 2:8–9

John 1:12

Notes

13 Assurance of Salvation

In him you also, when you heard the word of truth,
the gospel of your salvation, and believed in him,
were sealed with the promised Holy Spirit.
—Ephesians 1:13 (ESV)

Apostle Paul explained what occurred in the lives of the believers in Ephesus (Ephesians 1:13).

- First, they heard the Gospel message. What is the Gospel message? The Gospel message is the good news that Christ died for your sin. He was buried. He was raised from the dead (1 Corinthians 15:3–4).
- Second, they believed the Gospel message and were saved.
- Third, when they believed, they were immediately sealed with the promised Holy Spirit.

During Mother's life on earth, she heard the Gospel message. She believed it and was saved (1 Corinthians 15:3–4; Romans 10:9; Ephesians 2:8–9). At once, she was sealed with the Holy Spirit (Ephesians 1:13).

The instant you believe the Gospel message, you are sealed with the Holy Spirit, who is promised to you by the Father. Once you are saved, you can never lose your salvation. The seal cannot be broken. It is secure. Therefore, you belong to the Lord forever. You are sealed by the Holy Spirit for the day of redemption (Ephesians 4:30). Remember, the Holy Spirit is a gift to you after salvation.

Encouraging Bible Verses

John 5:24

John 3:36

John 10:28

John 6:37

John 11:26

John 6:47

1 John 5:11–13

Notes

Resources

The following resources are provided by AARP Family Caregiving. Visit AARP Caregiving Resource Center for information, tips, tools, and resources while caring for a loved one at www.aarp/caregiving, or call 877-333-5885. For Spanish resources, visit www.aarp.org/cuidar or call 888-971-2013.

AARP Advance Directive Forms
www.aarp.org/advancedirectives
Free, downloadable, state-specific, advance directive forms and instructions.

AARP Care Guides
www.aarp.org/careguides
Take the stress out of caregiving with these targeted, easy-to-use guides.

AARP Local Caregiver Resource Guides
www.aarp.org/caregiverresourceguides
Local resources that help make caregiving easier.

AARP Caregiving Tools
www.aarp.org/caregivingtools
AARP's suite of web-based tools will help you find services, keep track of health records, and more.

AARP Medicare Q&A Tool
www.aarp.org/MedicareQA
An easy-to-use online tool that provides answers to frequently asked questions about Medicare.

AARP Health Law Answers
www.healthlawanswers.org
An online tool designed to help you understand what the health-care law means for you and your family and where to go for information in your state.

AARP I Heart Caregivers
www.aarp.org/iheartcaregivers
Share your caregiving story and connect with others.

AARP Long-Term Care Cost Calculator
www.aarp.org/longtermcarecosts
Find and compare the costs of home care, assisted living and other services throughout the United States.

AARP Online Caregiving Community
www.aarp.org/caregivingcommunity
Join the community and connect with other caregivers like you.

Administration on Community Living (ACL)
www.acl.gov
This federal agency is responsible for advancing the concerns and interests of older people. The website has a variety of tools and information for older adults and family caregivers.

Alzheimer's Association
www.alz.org
800-272-3900
Resources, tools, and a twenty-four-hour helpline for people with Alzheimer's disease and their families.

American Cancer Society
www.cancer.org or 800-227-2345
From basic information about cancer and its causes to in-depth information on specific cancer types—including risk factors, early detection, diagnosis and treatment options.

American Diabetes Association
www.diabetes.org or 800-342-2383
Resources and research to prevent, cure, and manage diabetes.

American Heart Association
www.heart.org or 800-242-8721
Resources that will help you better care for someone who has heart disease or who has had a heart attack, heart surgery, or a stroke.

Argentum
www.argentum.org
Information and resources on assisted living options and how to find them.

Care.com
www.care.com
Improving the lives of families and caregivers by helping them connect in a reliable and easy way.

Caregiver Action Network
www.caregiveraction.org or 202-454-3970
Information, educational materials, and support for family caregivers.

Caring Info
www.caringinfo.org
A national engagement initiative to improve care at the end of life.

Eldercare Locator
www.eldercare.gov
800-677-1116
A public service of the US Administration on Aging that connects caregivers to local services and resources for older adults.

Elizabeth Dole Foundation
www.elizabethdolefoundation.org
Created to help American military caregivers by strengthening the services afforded to them through innovation, evidence-based research, and collaboration.

Family Caregiver Alliance
www.caregiver.org
800-445-8106
Tools and resources for family caregivers, including the Family Care Navigator, a state-by-state list of services and assistance.

Leading Age
www.leadingage.org
Consumer information on long-term care facilities, services, and how to access them.

Medicare
www.medicare.gov
The official U. S. government site for Medicare
800-633-4227
Provides information about the Medicare program and how to find Medicare plans and providers. Caregivers will also find a tool on the website to compare home health-care agencies and nursing homes.

National Academy of Elder Law Attorneys
www.naela.org
A professional association of attorneys who specialize in legal services for older adults and people with special needs.

Find information on legal issues affecting older adults and a database of elder law attorneys by state.

National Alliance for Caregiving
www.caregiving.org
This organization is dedicated to improving the quality of life for caregivers and those they care for through research, innovation, and advocacy.

National Alliance for Hispanic Health
www.healthyamericas.org
866-783-2645
The Hispanic Family Health Helpline and its Su Familia provide free and confidential health information for Hispanic families.

National Association for Home Care and Hospice
www.nahc.org
Provides consumer information on how to select a home care provider or hospice.

National Association of Home Builders
www.nahb.org/caps
800-368-5242
A web-based directory of certified aging-in-place specialists who can identify and/or provide home modifications that make a home accessible, safer, and more comfortable.

National Association of Social Workers
www.socialworkers.org
This organization maintains a directory of licensed social workers at www.helppro.com/nasw.

National Clearinghouse for Long-Term Care Information
www.longtermcare.gov
Information and tools used to help plan for long-term care needs.

National Hospice and Palliative Care Organization
www.nhpco.org
800-646-6460
Provides free consumer information on hospice care and puts the public in direct contact with hospice programs.

National Multiple Sclerosis Society
www.nationalmssociety.org
Offers resources and support to navigate the best life through the challenges of MS.

National Parkinson Foundation
www.parkinson.org
800-473-4636
Events, research progress, and resources for those affected by Parkinson's disease.

National Respite Network
www.archrespite.org
A service that helps people locate respite services.

NIH Senior Health
www.nihseniorhealth.gov
800-222-2225
Fact sheets from the US National Institutes of Health can be viewed online or ordered for free.

Rosalynn Carter Institute for Caregiving
www.rosalynncarter.org
Created to support caregivers, both family and professional, through the effort of advocacy, education, research, and service.

SAGECAP
www.sageusa.org/sagecap
An organization that provides counseling, information, support groups, and more to gay, lesbian, bisexual, and transgender caregivers.

Social Security Administration
www.ssa.gov
800-772-1213
Help and information on eligibility and benefits are available online, and phone help is available.

State Health Insurance Assistance Program (SHIP)
www.shiptacenter.org
877-839-2675
Your local SHIP offers one-on-one counseling assistance for people with Medicare and their families.

The Conversation Project
www.theconversationproject.org
Created to help people talk about their wishes for end-of-life care.

Veterans Affairs
www.caregiver.va.gov
855-260-3274
Provides supports and services for families caring for veterans. Connects caregivers with local caregiver support programs for veterans.

Village to Village Network
www.vtvnetwork.org
An organization that helps communities start villages, which are membership-based groups that respond to the needs of older people within a geographic area. Find villages across the United States online.

2-1-1
www.211.org
A free and confidential service that helps people across North America find the local resources they need.

Be an empowered caregiver
with powerful resources.

Notes

Let everything that has breath praise
the LORD. Praise the LORD.
—Psalm 150:6 (NIV)

Notes

Give thanks to the LORD, for he is
good; his love endures forever.
—1 Chronicles 16:34 (NIV)

Notes

Give unto the LORD the glory due unto his name;
worship the LORD in the beauty of holiness.
—Psalm 29:2 (KJV)

Notes

The earth is the LORD's, and everything
in it, the world, and all who live in it.
—Psalm 24:1 (NIV)

Notes

For our light and momentary troubles are achieving
for us an eternal glory that far outweighs them all.
—2 Corinthians 4:17 (NIV)

Notes

While we look not at the things which are
seen, but at the things which are not seen: for
the things which are seen are temporal; but
the things which are not seen are eternal.
—2 Corinthians 4:18 (KJV)

Notes

This is My commandment, that you love
one another as I have loved you.
—John 15:12 (NKJV)

Notes

Let your light so shine before men, that
they may see your good works, and glorify
your Father which is in heaven.
—Matthew 5:16 (KJV)

Notes

Do not love the world or the things in
the world. If anyone loves the world, the
love of the Father is not in him.
—1 John 2:15 (ESV)

Notes

Love the LORD your God with all your heart and
with all your soul and with all your strength.
—Deuteronomy 6:5 (NIV)

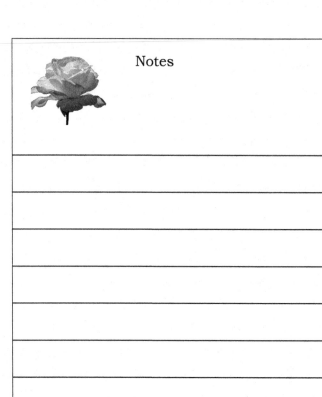

Notes

But without faith it is impossible to please
Him, for he who comes to God must believe
that He is, and that He is a rewarder
of those who diligently seek Him.
—Hebrews 11:6 (NKJV)

Notes

Now faith is the substance of things hoped
for, the evidence of things not seen.
—Hebrews 11:1 (KJV)

Notes

But these are written that you may believe that
Jesus is the Messiah, the Son of God, and that
by believing you may have life in his name.
—John 20:31 (NIV)

Notes

You believe because you have seen me. Blessed
are those who believe without seeing me.
—John 20:29 (NLT)

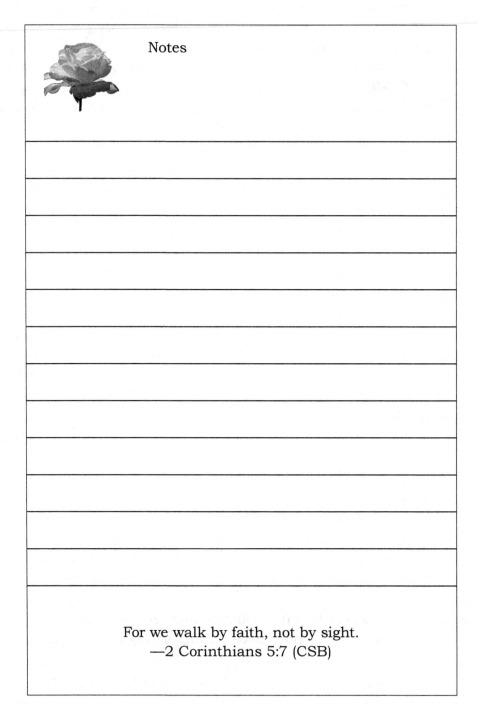

Notes

For we walk by faith, not by sight.
—2 Corinthians 5:7 (CSB)

Notes

In the same way, I tell you, there is joy
in the presence of the angels of God
over one sinner who repents.
—Luke 15:10 (NASB)

In Memoriam

Brothers and sisters, we do not want you to be uniformed
about those who sleep in death, so that you do not
grieve like the rest of mankind, who have no hope.
—1 Thessalonians 4:13 (NIV)

You left us with powerful, precious memories—your faith, your love for God, your prayers, your advice and guidance, your support, your gentleness, your strength, your discipline, your teaching and training; your love, your joy, and your laughter.

Our souls ache for you.
Nothing is the same.
In God's perfect timing,
We will gaze upon your face again.

Until we meet again.
—Lonnie Jr., Wilhelminia, Margaret, and Carolyn

Lonnie Hill, Sr.

Sunset: February 8, 2003

Dad was a decorated World War II veteran. He was the recipient of the Victory Medal, the EAMET Service Medal, and the Good Conduct Medal.

You were our rock, our solid foundation. You touched countless lives with your caring, giving heart. We are blessed God created you, and we are honored to call you our handsome, strong dad.

Olga Hill

Sunset: January 13, 2015

Blessed by you, our beloved
A mother's love
A mother's prayers
A mother's light
A mother's example
Forever there
Blessed, our beloved
God created you

Evelyn Hill
Sunset: October 9, 1994

I will always remember your laughter, sister-in-law: warm, full of joy, and from the heart. The separation is difficult, but the time we will spend together with the Lord is eternal.

Margaret Dixon

Sunset: February 23, 2019

Through jubilant times, trials, sickness, and death, we comprehended what it meant to have each other. We shared so much love, so much joy, so much laughter, so many prayers, so much pain, so much sorrow and so many tears.

You were an amazing and incredible sister. You were astute and beautiful, and you had exceptional gifts and talents. You loved the Lord and tried to live your life according to His Word. Lonnie Jr., Wilhelminia, and I miss you, but we will see you again, along with Dad and Mother—forever together with our Lord and Savior, Jesus Christ, and all the saints. Your sweet, fond, and joyful memories will remain with us until we meet again.

Niasha Hill

Sunset: April 4, 2020

Often I reflect on the treasured, warm memories we shared. You were shrewd, caring, gorgeous, glamorous, an excellent encourager, and a powerful prayer partner. I will always remember these words: "May I pray for you, Aunt Carolyn?" I miss your sweet voice, but I will hear it again. You would tell me, "I know Jesus." Now, you are with Jesus. Praise the Lord.

Jesus is the way to heaven (John 14:6).
He is the door to heaven (John 10:9).

One way—John 14:6
One door—John 10:9
No other way
No other entrance
Jesus Christ only

We would prefer to be away from the body and at home with the Lord (2 Corinthians 5:8 CSB).

About the Author

Carolyn Harrison attracts the reader to her with her passionate and powerful writings as a caregiver. Her writings convey encouragement, inspiration, love, the promises of God, and hope. After the demise of her beloved mother, she was motivated and led by the Holy Spirit to pen her recent book, *For Such a Time as This: A Caregiver's Encouragement.*

Carolyn retired from Hamilton County Schools in 2008, completing thirty years of service. She was a caregiver to her beloved mother from 2003 to 2015. In 2016, she began her personal Gospel tract ministry.

Carolyn is a 1975 graduate of Bethune-Cookman University, Daytona Beach, Florida, where she received her bachelor of science degree. While in attendance at Bethune-Cookman University, she became a member of Delta Sigma Theta Sorority and of Pi Omega Pi, a scholastic honor society recognizing academic achievement among students in the field of business education. She graduated from the University of Tennessee at Chattanooga (UTC) in Chattanooga, Tennessee, in 1981, where she received her master of education degree. While attending UTC, she became a member of Kappa Delta Pi, an honor society in education. Her professional and nonpartisan organizations include Chattanooga-Hamilton County Retired Teachers Association, Tennessee Retired Teachers Association, National Retired Teachers Association, and American Association of Retired Persons (AARP). She received special recognition as a Legendary Lady of Merit, awarded by Tennessee State University National Alumni Association Chattanooga Chapter.

When Carolyn is not devoting time to her personal ministry, she enjoys trying new things—writing, landscaping, floral arrangement, and playing the organ.

Carolyn was born and raised in LaGrange, Georgia, and she currently resides in Chattanooga, Tennessee, with her spouse, Charlie.

> I count all things but loss for the excellency of the knowledge of Christ Jesus my Lord. (Philippians 3:8 KJV)